This Book belongs to: Frances Louise Elson

Vogel, A.
The ballet book for little dancers
1. Ballet dancing – Juvenile literature
I. Title II. Sievert, Heidi III. Das
Grosse Buch für die Kleine Tänzerin. **English**
792.8'2 GV1788

ISBN 0-7136-2611-9

For:

Kolja, Claus, Antje, Peter, Inger, Heiner, Rosemarie, Michael, Sabine, Elisabeth, Max, Helmut, Wolfgang, Siggi, Gertrud, Sebastian, Ulle, Gudula, Stefanie, Axel, Toni, Hugo, Erika, Lutz, Monika, Boris, David, Ulla, Andrea, Uta, Krystof, Hilde, Katrinchen, Lotte, Huck, Julika, Benjamin, Katinka, Daniela, Katrin, Marco, Robert, Heike, Helga, Carl-Wilhelm, Blacky, Martin, Lucie, Vera, Carl, Eva, Patrick, Claus, Brigitte, Markus, Nicolai, Marc, Tanja, Kay, Irmtraut, Anita, Herlinde, Dietmar, Vivi, Barbara, Dieter, Jurgen, Christl, Christian, Edith, Philipp, Matthias, Florian, Jan, Klas, Heidi, Hermann, Emil, Mascha, Collin, Cay, Britta, Frederik, Anna, Dagmar, Walter, Uschi, Reimer, Kirsten, Tim, John, Ilse, Nils, Nienke, Hielian, Frank, Pieter, Schnasi, Iris, Gisela, Isabell, Inga, Fritz, Barbel, Julia, Josefine, Cornelius, Rolf, Gabi, Heinz, Geka, Ingrid, Karin, Thomas, Beate, Diana, Ralf, George, Bruni, Jochen, Ali, Uwe, Laura, Josi, Micky, Lilly, Bertel, Edgar, Horst, Icki, Jana, Astrid, Annette, Adelie, Charly, Claudine, Renate, Arno, Ulrike, Susanne, Tassilo, Manfred, Jessica, Dorothee, Hans, Bernd, Gro, Hansi, Linn, Helma, Puppa, Volker, Claes, Meike, Inka, Ellen, Felix, Doris, Patricia, Pia, Franz, Carla, Brigitta, Sven, Nina, Lisa, Swantje, Cora, Alexander, Henry, Heino, Elke, Gerold, Andreas, Angela, Angelika, Beatrix, Pit, Rosi, Jeannette, Christiane, Christine, Tina, Melanie, Claudia, Bruno, Illiana, Jupp, Madeleine, Mo, Kaspar, Moritz, Paul-Clemens, Schitti, Daniel, Natalie, Diemut, Marc-Daniel, Valerie, Frederic, Esther, Denise, Sarah, Kirsten, Alexa, Leo, Tessa, Franziska, Gudrun, Judith, Julian, Ortrud, Cornelia, Martina, Thekla, Silvia, Majja, Verena, Ossy, Nika, Annika, Maren, Bastian, Natascha, Judy, Till, Michaela, Marion, Kajo, Ingeborg, Petra, Birgit, Karola, Christa, Imme, Ina, Irene, Karoline, Marina, Sonja, Gabriele, Christoph, Itta, Karsten, Karl-Georg, Anne, Anja, Christa, Dick, Werner, Lis, Katja, Graziela, Pia, Larissa, Melanie, Tilman, Karsten, Christa, Rupert, Michelle, Juli, Claire, Colette, Ines, Christine, Claudia, Heike, Anita, Helga, Johanna, Dimitri, Gudrun, Andreina, Mira, Nicole, Ulf, Marco, Regina, Sascha, Ulrike, Ari-Daniel, Klaus-Dieter, Judith, Tilla and:

....

First published
in Great Britain 1984 by
A & C Black (Publishers) Ltd,
35 Bedford Row, London WC1R 4JH.
Second impression 1986.
Originally published in Germany 1979
by Coppenrath Verlag with the title
"Das Grosse Buch für die Kleine Tänzerin".
© Copyright 1979 by F Coppenrath Verlag,
Martinistrasse 2, D-4400 Münster,
West Germany.

All rights reserved.
No part of this publication may
be extracted. Use of the
illustrations requires the express
permission of the publisher.
Printed and bound in Spain
by Mateu Cromo Artes
Graficas, S.A.

ISBN 0-7136-2611-9

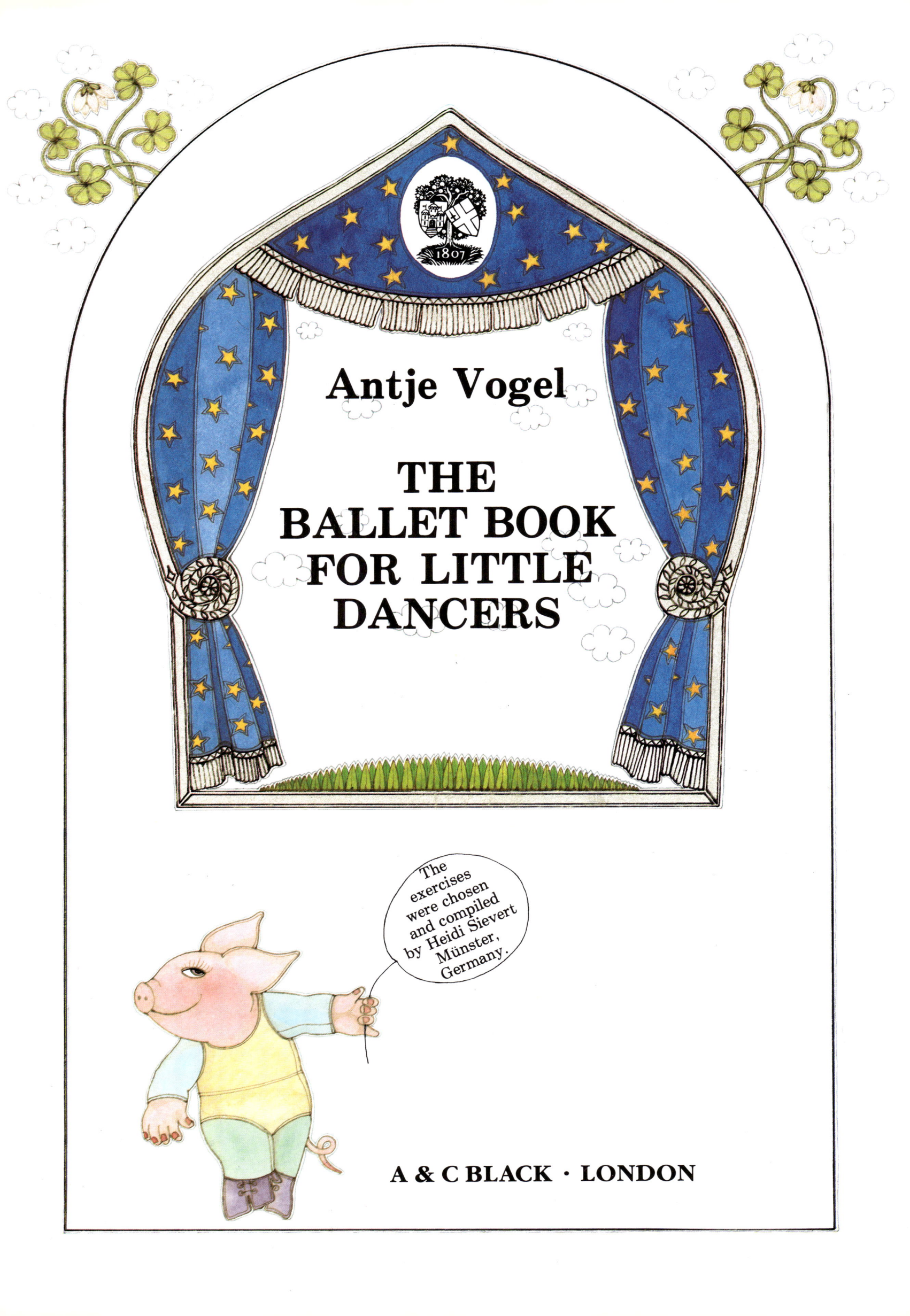

Antje Vogel

THE BALLET BOOK FOR LITTLE DANCERS

The exercises were chosen and compiled by Heidi Sievert Münster, Germany.

A & C BLACK · LONDON

Dear ＿＿＿＿＿＿＿＿,

In this book you will find all the exercises for an hour's ballet lesson. There are exercises for loosening up, exercises at the barre and exercises in the centre — in other words, without holding on.

So — you are ready to begin . . .

Even if you don't go to a ballet school it will be fun to practise the loosening up exercises. My son Kolja can do them and he's only five. He watched me while I was doing the drawings and immediately tried them all.

Ballet is fun! Not only that, an hour's exercises will use every muscle in the body. That makes ballet an ideal sport for children and adults alike.

Have fun!

Yours,

Antje Vogel

What do I need and when?

The tutu, a stage costume, may be needed for a performance.

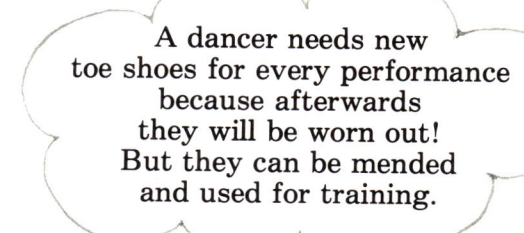

A dancer needs new toe shoes for every performance because afterwards they will be worn out! But they can be mended and used for training.

Leotard

Make your own!

Legwarmers
2 knitting needles Nr.8. Bits of old wool. Cast on about 40 stitches. Knit 2 and purl 2 until work measures about 30 cms. Cast off and sew the side seams together.

Toe shoes have a reinforced toe cap and a hard sole. You should not start to toe-dance before the age of 10-12. Before that age foot joints would be under too much strain.

Tights

Legwarmers

Softs

You start ballet school around the age of 6 and jazz ballet from about the age of 15.

Loosening up exercises

1

Sit on the floor, feet together, knees apart. Bounce knees gently up and down while counting up to 8.

Then let your knees rest and loosely bounce your head toward your feet while counting to 8.

Now stretch your arms way up over your head. Make your back long and straight. Stretch your sides from the waist and count to 8. Gently drop your head to your feet, keeping your back round and count to 8.

Repeat both exercises alternately (one after the other).

2

Sitting on the floor stretch both legs in front of you. Extend arms over legs and keep back very straight.

Then pull in tummy, round your back, shoulders forward again, tighten your bottom and bounce towards your toes.

Sit up, and with a rounded back roll back till you're lying on the floor and quickly...

...come up again with a straight back, keeping your legs flat on the floor if you can!

Or else lift your legs to raise yourself up.

That's fun!

Lie on the floor, legs straight, arms to the side.

3

Arch your back, leaving shoulders, head, bottom and legs on the floor.

Then press your back to the floor, allowing your knees to come up.

Or else arch your back, breathe in, count to 4. Straighten your back, breathe out, count to 4.

What is where?

- Shoulder
- Ribs
- Elbow
- Right arm
- Left arm
- Waist
- Tummy
- Hip
- Left leg
- Right leg
- Knee
- Shin
- Calf
- Instep
- Point
- Ball
- Heel

4

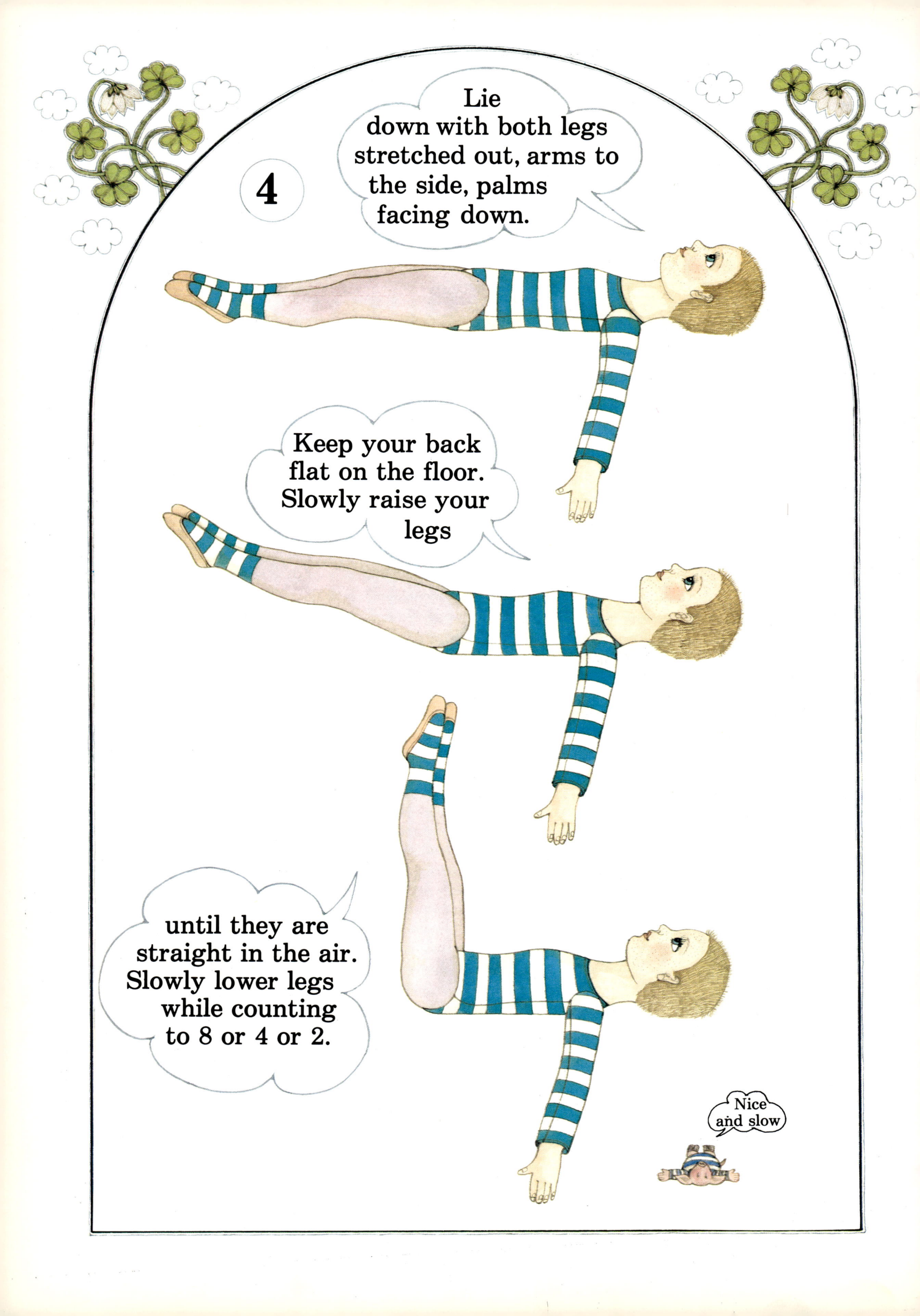

Lie down with both legs stretched out, arms to the side, palms facing down.

Keep your back flat on the floor. Slowly raise your legs

until they are straight in the air. Slowly lower legs while counting to 8 or 4 or 2.

Nice and slow

Then
raise your right leg
and bring it slowly down,
almost to the floor.
Repeat 8 times and do
the same with your
left leg.

Hard work!

5

Sit with your legs wide apart, the upper part of your body very straight and arms up.

Bounce towards your right leg with both hands towards the right foot. Count up to 8.

Do the same towards the left foot.

Next, bend forward with a straight back and pull forward rather than leaning towards the floor. Count to 8.

Then round your back, nose to the floor, and unroll till your back is straight. Arms high.

By the way . . .

The story goes that in about 1824 the ballet master Filippo Taglioni invented toe-dancing for his daughter Maria in the hope of distracting attention from her long nose!

And Maria Taglioni really did become a very famous dancer.

6

Crouch down with
your hands on the floor
in front of your feet.
Feet together.

Bounce 4 times while crouching.
Then straighten legs, keeping hands
on the floor as long as you can.
Repeat the whole exercise 4 or 8 times.
After the last time straighten up very slowly
— unroll one vertebra at a time
till your whole body is straight.

Keep
legs nice and
straight.

7

Stand with your legs parallel and slightly apart. Body straight.

Now breathe out, lowering yourself still further, breathe in, round your back again, breathe out.

Roll your head down, then your shoulders until your back is nicely rounded and your body hangs loosely.

Come up with a straight back, bringing your arms up at the same time, and then . . .

loosely drop forward.

Breathe out again, straighten your back and stretch far forward.

Don't keep all your weight on the heels but spread it over the whole foot.

Wrong! Right!

8

Stand with your legs parallel, feet slightly apart, arms to the side.

With a straight back, bend forward until the upper part of your body is horizontal to the floor. Keep arms to the side.

Now swing upper body down, arms together. Back rounded.

Come back to a horizontal position, back straight, arms to the side.

Repeat 8 times, then come up with a straight back.

By the way . . .

In ballet class you should never wear jewellery, watches, baggy clothes or have loose hair.

Because when you turn you can't see anything.

Because your ballet teacher can't see whether you're pulling in your tummy and straightening your legs.

Right.

Wrong.

9

Stand with your legs parallel and slightly apart. Hold left arm high above your head, right arm to the side.

Reaching with your left hand, bend to the right, tummy pulled in. Don't forget to pull in your bottom too! Bounce 4 or 8 times, then . . .

fall forward. Back is round and arms hang down, legs slightly bent.

Now straighten legs, bend over to the right and straighten up again. Do the same on the left side.

10

Stand with left leg behind right leg, toes pointing to the floor.

Pull in your bottom!

Now bounce left heel to the floor twice while bending the front leg and keeping the back one straight.

On the count of 3, kick back leg forward. Back stays straight. On the count of 4 set leg down.

Repeat the whole exercise 8 times on the left and 8 times on the right side. Count to 4 each time.

The 5 Positions of the Feet

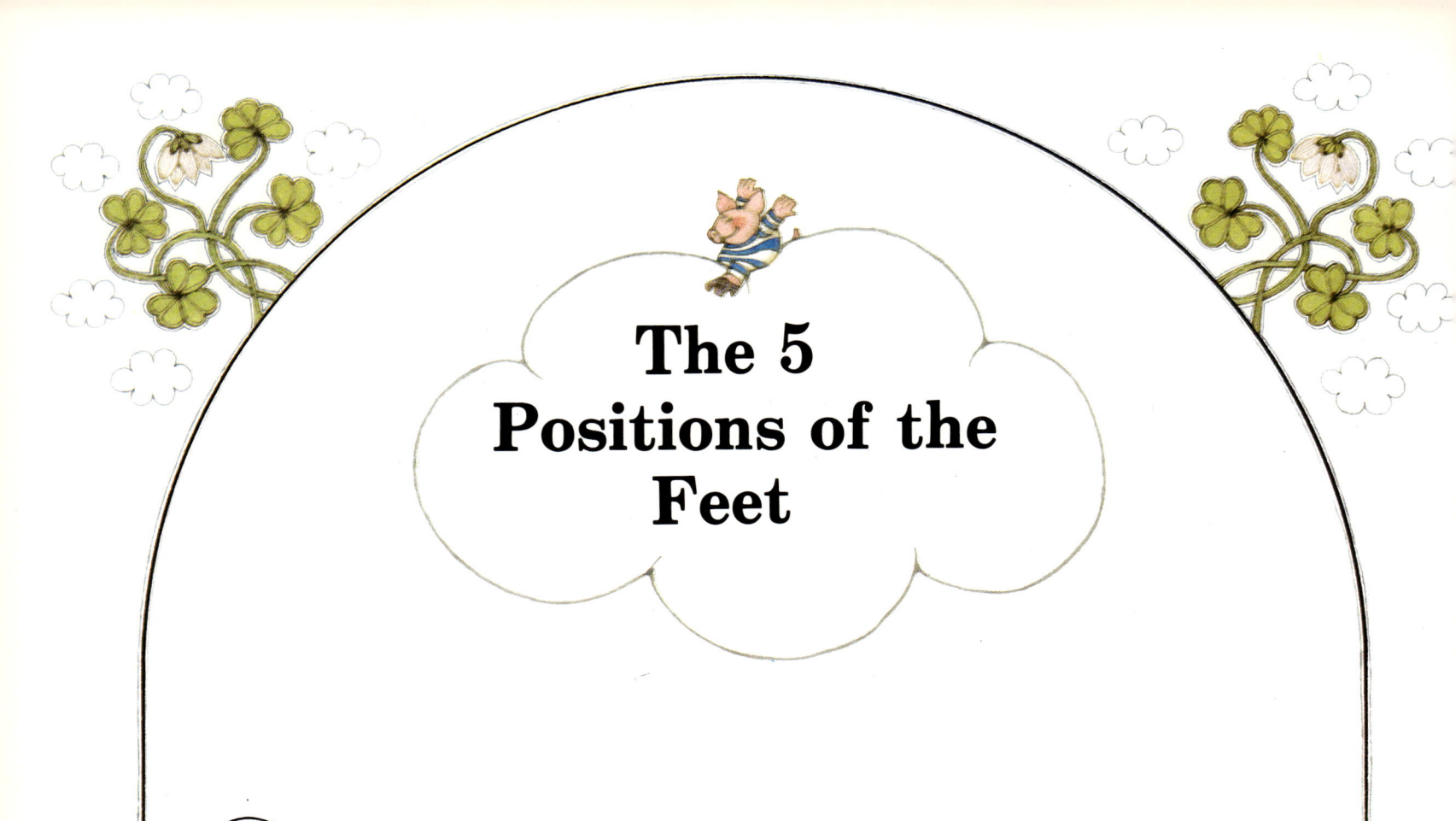

1. With heels together turn your feet out as far as your thighs will turn. When bending your knees, they should be over your toes. All your toes should lie flat on the floor. The outer edge of the foot should carry more weight and the instep should be raised.

Very important as otherwise the knees would be damaged and it doesn't look so nice.

2. Turn thighs outward again with feet 1-1½ foot-lengths apart.

3. Put one foot halfway in front of the other with the heel of the front foot pressed against the arch of the back foot.

Beginners should only practise these three positions.

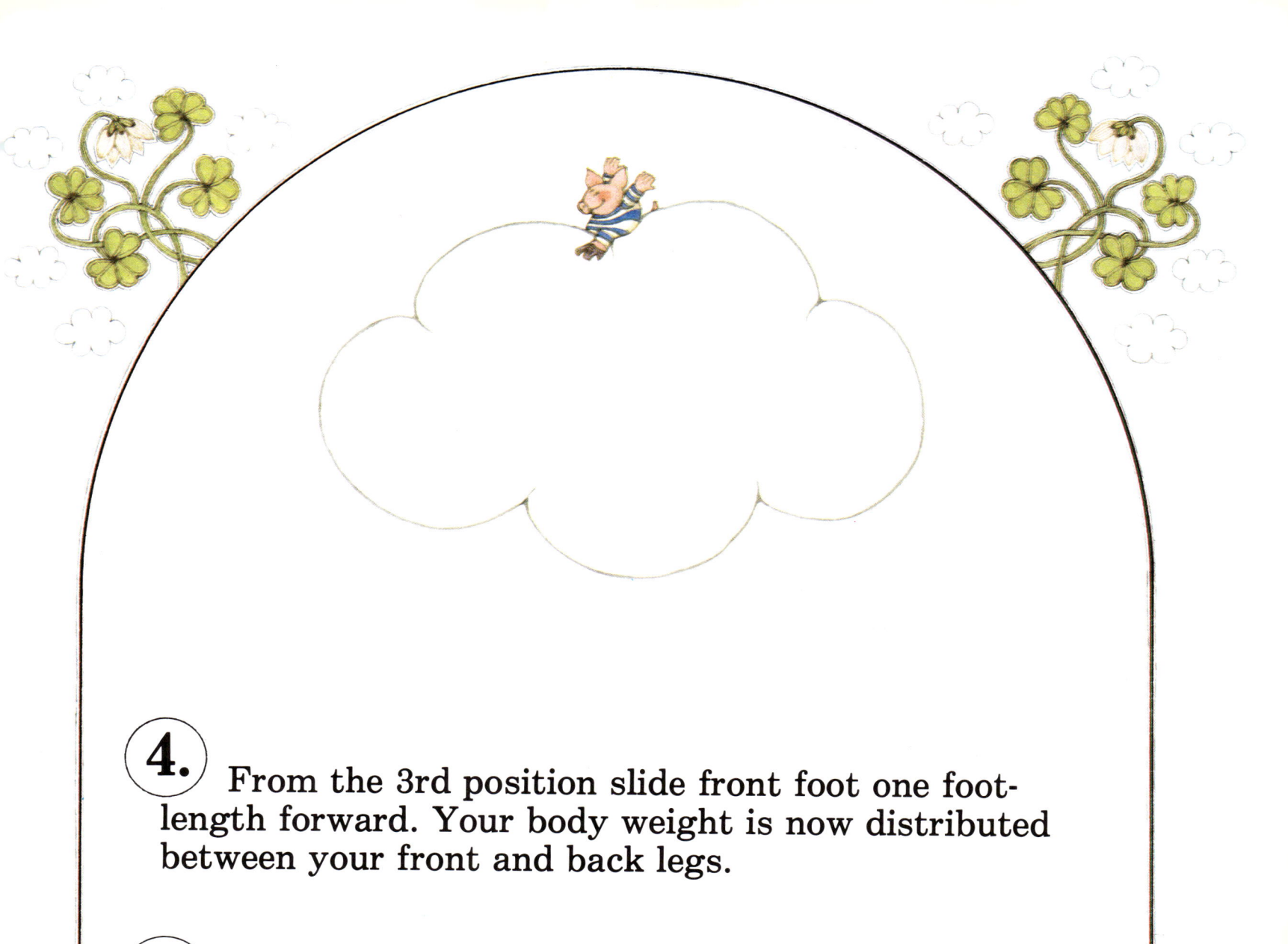

4. From the 3rd position slide front foot one foot-length forward. Your body weight is now distributed between your front and back legs.

5. Like the 3rd position except that the feet are more crossed. For the 5th position you must be well turned out from the hips, otherwise you stand flat-footed and put too much strain on your knees — and that's not healthy.

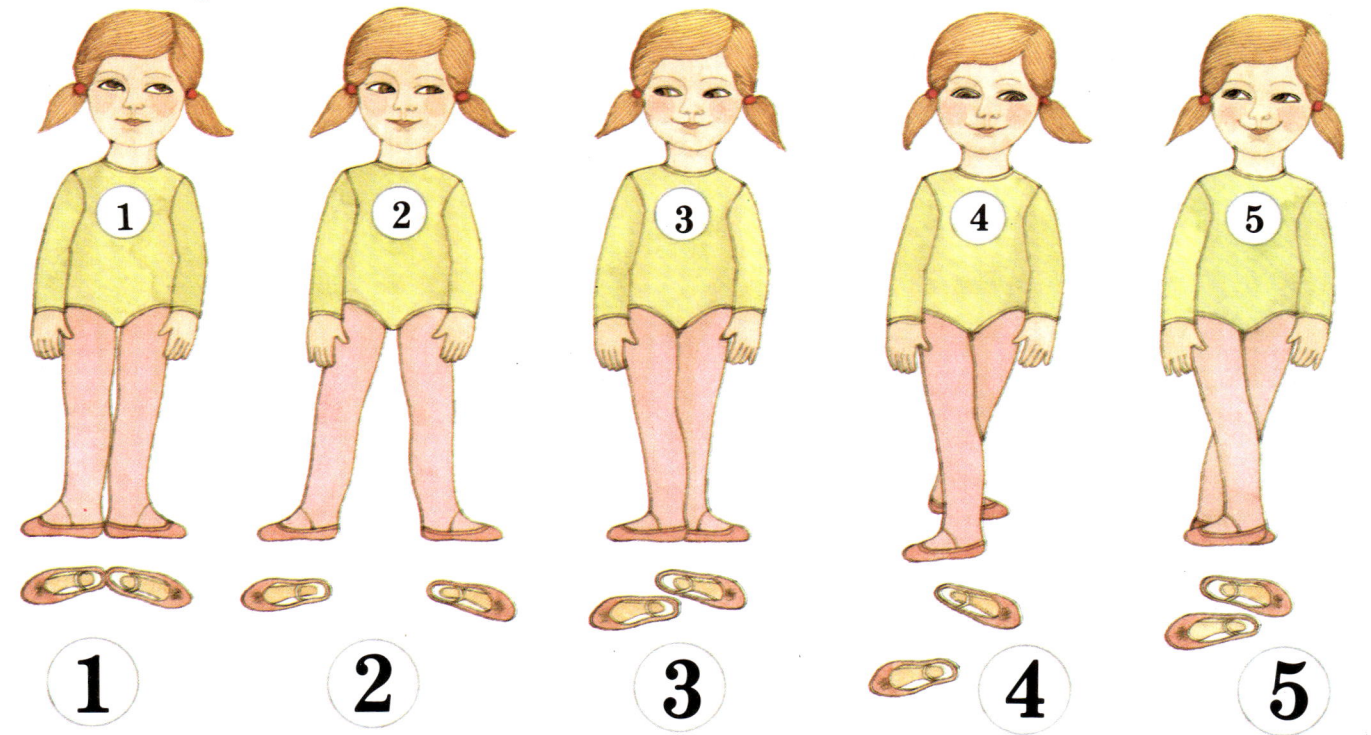

1   2   3   4   5

1   2   3   4   5

Exercises at the Barre

à la barre

Rest both hands loosely on the barre. Elbows in front of the body. Feet in 1st position.

For a demi-plié bend knees, making sure they are exactly over your toes. Heels stay flat on the floor. Back straight — don't let your bottom stick out.

You can also do the pliés with one hand on the barre. First right, then left.

(1) **Plié**

By the way . . .

This is the right way to stand at the barre: one hand is placed loosely on the barre — right in front of your body. Arm is almost completely straight. Push your bottom down and draw your tummy in – that straightens your spine. Now stretch your neck upwards and lift your head.

Bend your knees further down into a grand-plié lifting your heels off the floor as far as necessary. Come up again into a demi-plié, quickly drop your heels on to the floor and straighten your legs.

Don't go so low to the ground that you're sitting on your heels.

Pliés are done one after another in all 5 positions. In a demi-plié the heels should always stay flat on the floor. In a grand-plié they should stay flat only in the 2nd position. Knees are straight over the toes. Don't go so low that your bottom touches the ground.

2
Battement tendu

With the right hand on the barre, the left foot is working. With the left hand on the barre, the right foot is working.

1st position, one hand on the barre. Always use the outer leg. The inside leg is very straight.

Slide foot forward keeping leg very stiff. Ball of foot stays on the floor, heel pushed forward.

Continue sliding foot forward and straighten your leg. Do the same backwards, first with your foot half-pointed and then setting down your heel.

Keep the upper part of your body and hips still.

A battement tendu is done in this order: to the front, to the side, to the back, to the side. Then turn around with the other hand on the barre, and do the same with the other leg.

Do the same to the back. When sliding your foot make sure that the heel faces the floor. Slide the outer edge of your foot from the toes via the ball back into the 1st position in one neat movement.

The same to the side.

3

Battement tendu jeté

Slide the right leg forward as in a battement tendu but then raise the point of your foot about 20 cms off the floor, no higher. Don't swing your leg loosely but move powerfully right to the tips of your toes — just as if you were striking a match.

To the front, to the side, to the back, to the side. Always slide back into the 1st position. Repeat on the left side

4
An in-between exercise to strengthen the foot

Feet are next to each other i.e. parallel.

Left foot half pointed.

Pointed, half pointed, flat. Then your right foot, and so on. Keep changing.

The same in 1st position.

Half pointed, pointed, half pointed, flat. Unroll foot smoothly.

Keep changing from right to left. Hold onto the barre.

5
Rond de jambe à terre

Doing a rond de jambe is like drawing a half circle on the floor with a straight leg whereby the foot is pulled along the outer edge of the circle through into the 1st position. From the front to the side, to the back = 'en dehors' From the back to the side to the front = 'en dedans'. First with the right leg, then turn round, right hand on the barre and work with your left leg.

1st position.

Slide the right leg forward.

Bring it to the side.

Draw a half circle to the back.

Again to the side and forward.

6 Passé

From the 3rd position bring the outer leg up through half point along the supporting leg up to the knee.

The raised leg is pushed to the side. Careful — keep the supporting leg in position. Don't let it turn inward.

Then slide the pointed foot along the back of the supporting leg back into 3rd position. And from the back bring it up to the knee, then down in front.

7
Developpé

From the 3rd position, bring leg up through a passé and straighten out in front of you. Back must be straight. Keep the knee of supporting leg pulled up.

Then through a passé bring the leg back into the 3rd position.

Do the same to the side — passé, straighten leg to the side, knee facing upwards, not to the front. Passé, slide down the back of leg into 3rd position.

Now to the back. Passé, stretch your leg to the back. Keep your knee high. Don't let the upper part of your body lean forward. Tummy pulled in. Passé, close in the back, and repeat to the side.

Turn round and do the whole exercise with the other leg.

8

Grand Battement

3rd Position. Kick the right leg forward as high as you can. Both the supporting leg and the working leg are very straight. Back is straight. And so leg out, leg in – into 3rd position.

Now the same to the side, knee facing upwards, three to the front, three to the back.

To the back. Chest out, head up. Again to the side. Then turn round, other hand on the barre, and kick the other leg.

A rather fast movement!

By the way . . .

This is what a dancer looked like 150 years ago.

Maria Taglioni. April 23rd 1804 — April 24th 1884

The Positions of the Arms

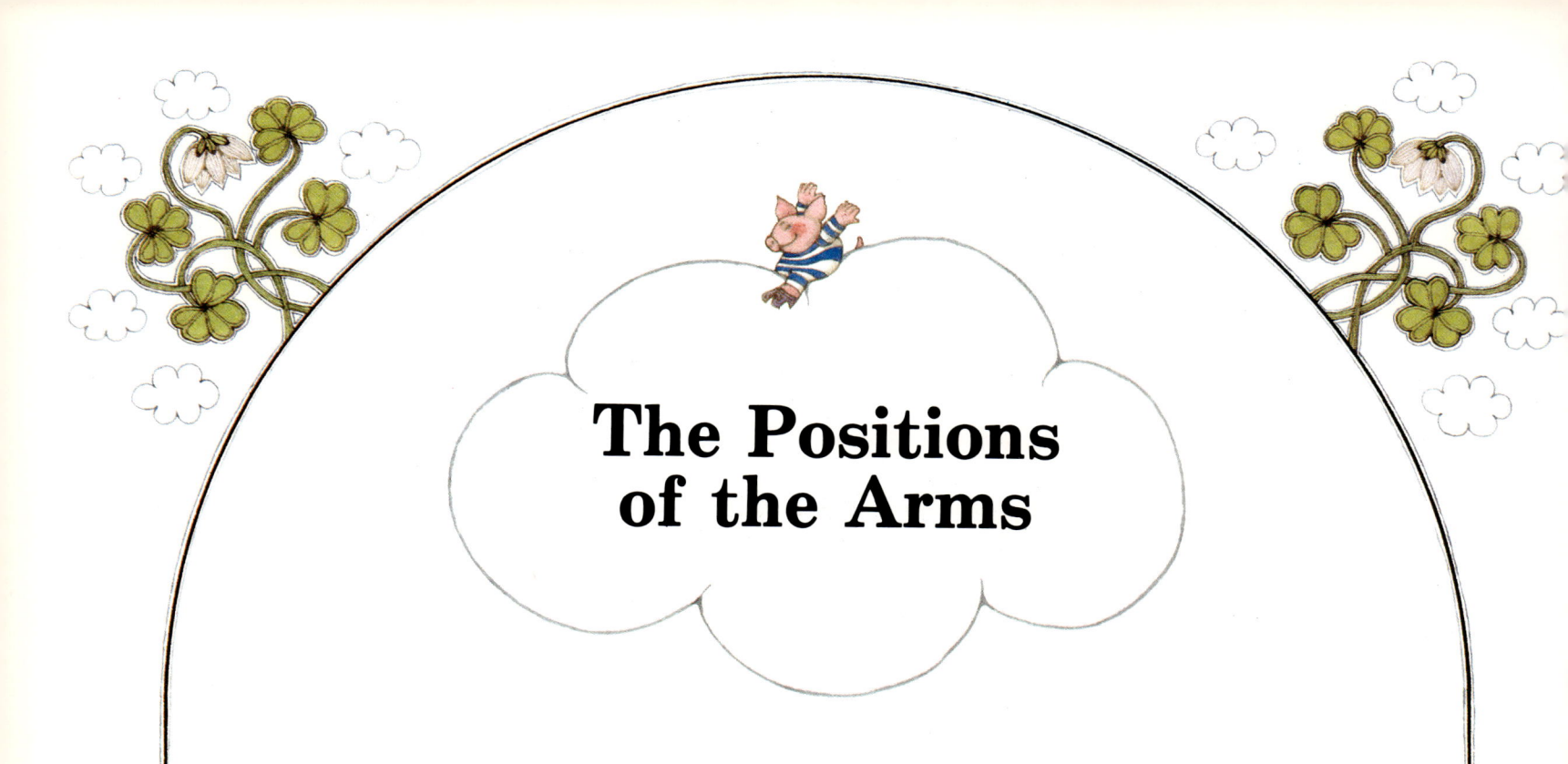

Both arms down and gently curved, with fingers almost touching. Elbows slightly raised. This is the basic position or 'préparation'.

All the exercises have French names because French is the 'ballet language'.

For 1st position
raise both arms in the basic position
to chest height. Open arms to the side into
2nd position, but not too far back. Always keep the arms in front of your body otherwise you may have an arched back. You must feel the tension from one hand through the back to the other hand — without interruption! Don't draw your shoulder blades together and don't let your shoulders fall forward. Now, raise your elbows towards the back, turn hands towards the front, keeping fingers together and bring both arms above your head into 3rd position.

Préparation

① ② ③

Now the fingers almost touch again, arms are not directly over the head but slightly to the front, shoulders stay low.

Centre practice

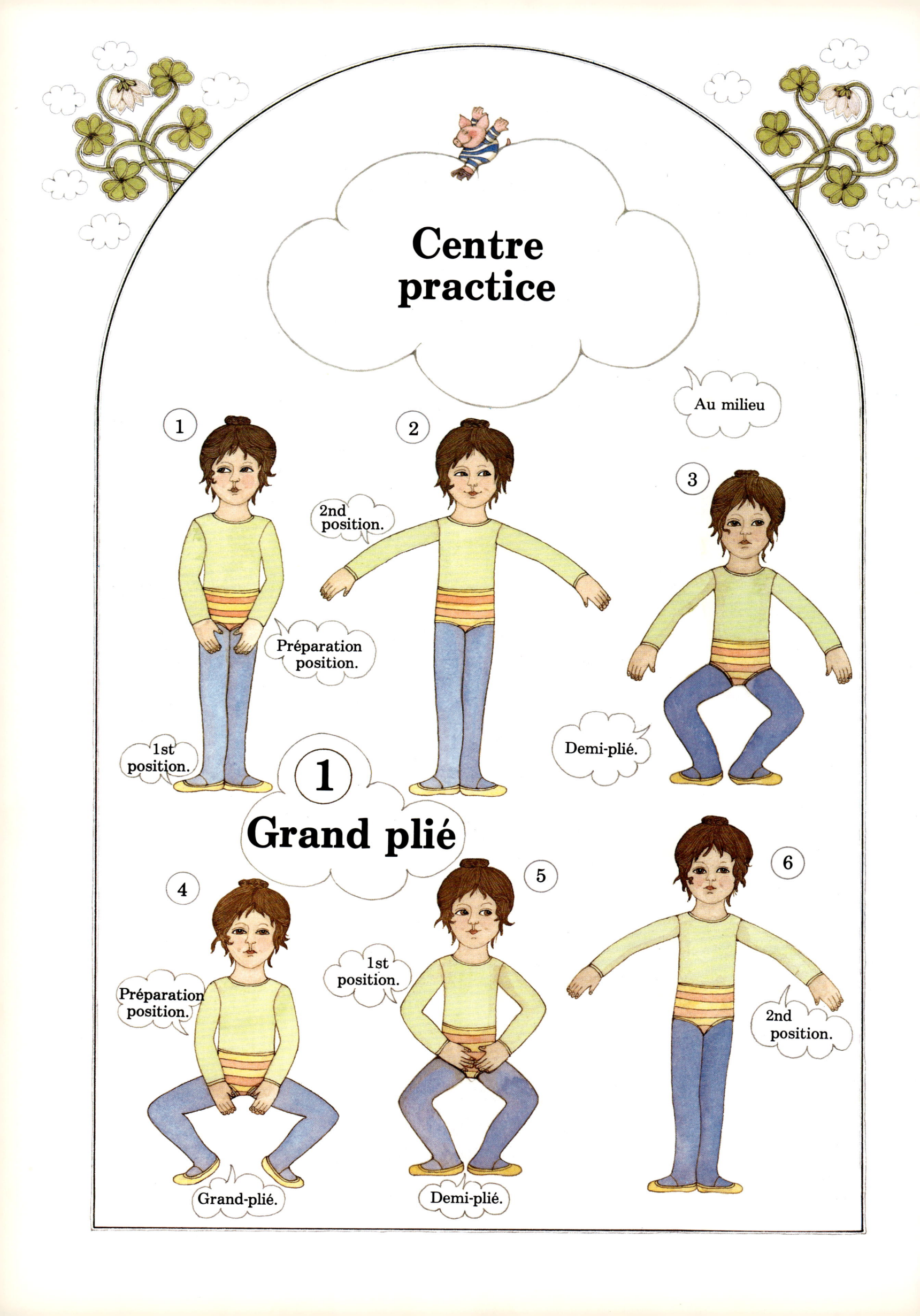

1 Grand plié

1. 1st position.
2. Préparation position. 2nd position.
3. Demi-plié. Au milieu
4. Préparation position. Grand-plié.
5. 1st position. Demi-plié.
6. 2nd position.

2 Relevé

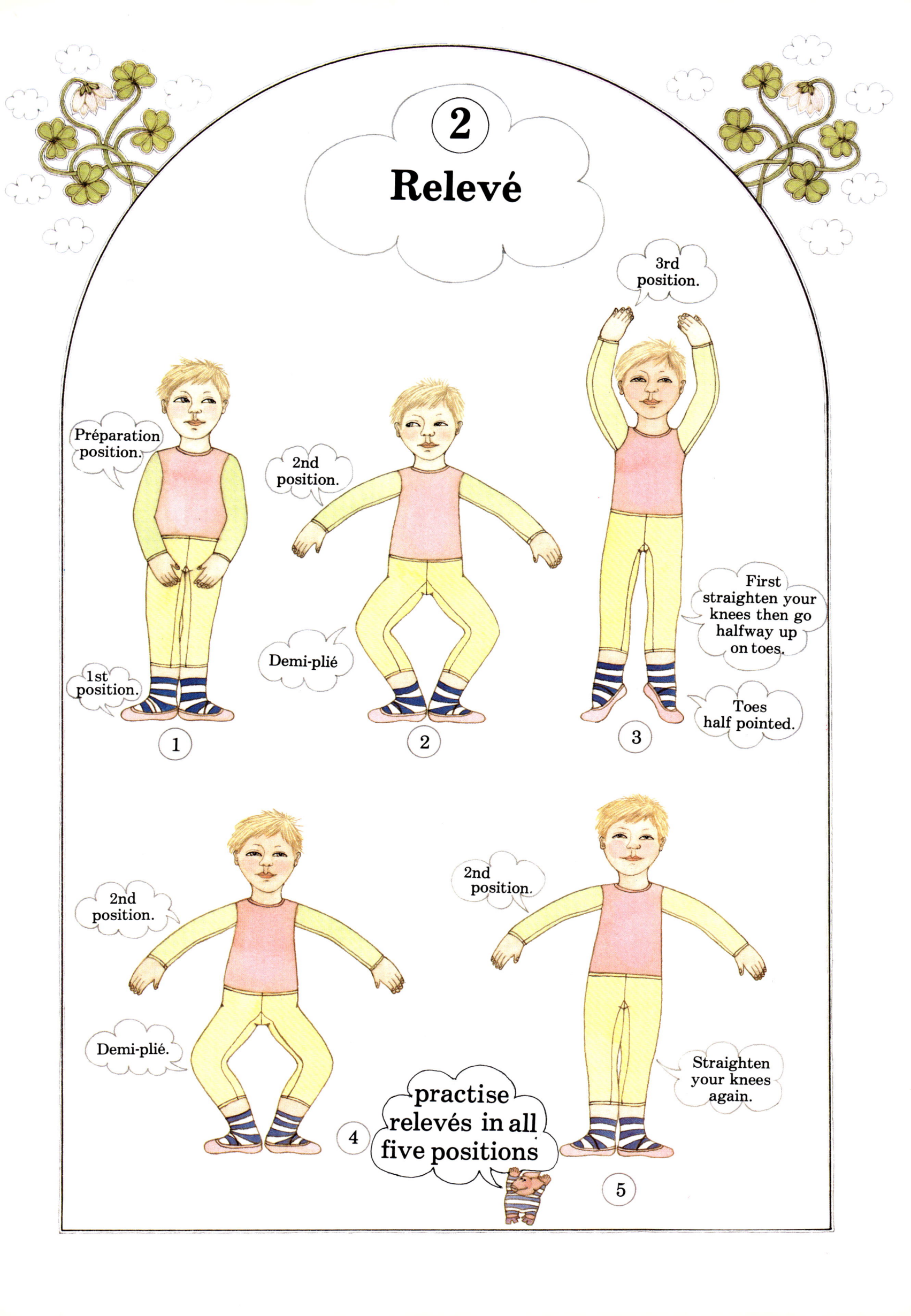

1. Préparation position. 1st position.
2. 2nd position. Demi-plié
3. 3rd position. First straighten your knees then go halfway up on toes. Toes half pointed.
4. 2nd position. Demi-plié.
5. 2nd position. Straighten your knees again.

practise relevés in all five positions

③ Relevé with passé

1 — Préparation position. 3rd position, right foot in front.

2 — 2nd position. Demi-plié.

3 — 3rd position. Passé. half pointed.

4 — 2nd position. Demi-plié. 3rd position, left foot in front.

5 — The same on the left foot. Right foot passé, left foot half pointed.

4
Pas de bourrée

3rd position, right foot front. Raise left leg to the calf, at the same time doing a demi-plié with the right leg.

Now drop the back leg in a relevé and raise your front leg to half point. Raise right arm to the front and bring it in over your head.

The front leg still in relevé goes into 2nd position.

Then bring the left leg forward in a demi-plié into 3rd position. Straighten your legs. If you now have the left leg in front, you've done it right.

And now continue to the left.

5
Arabesque

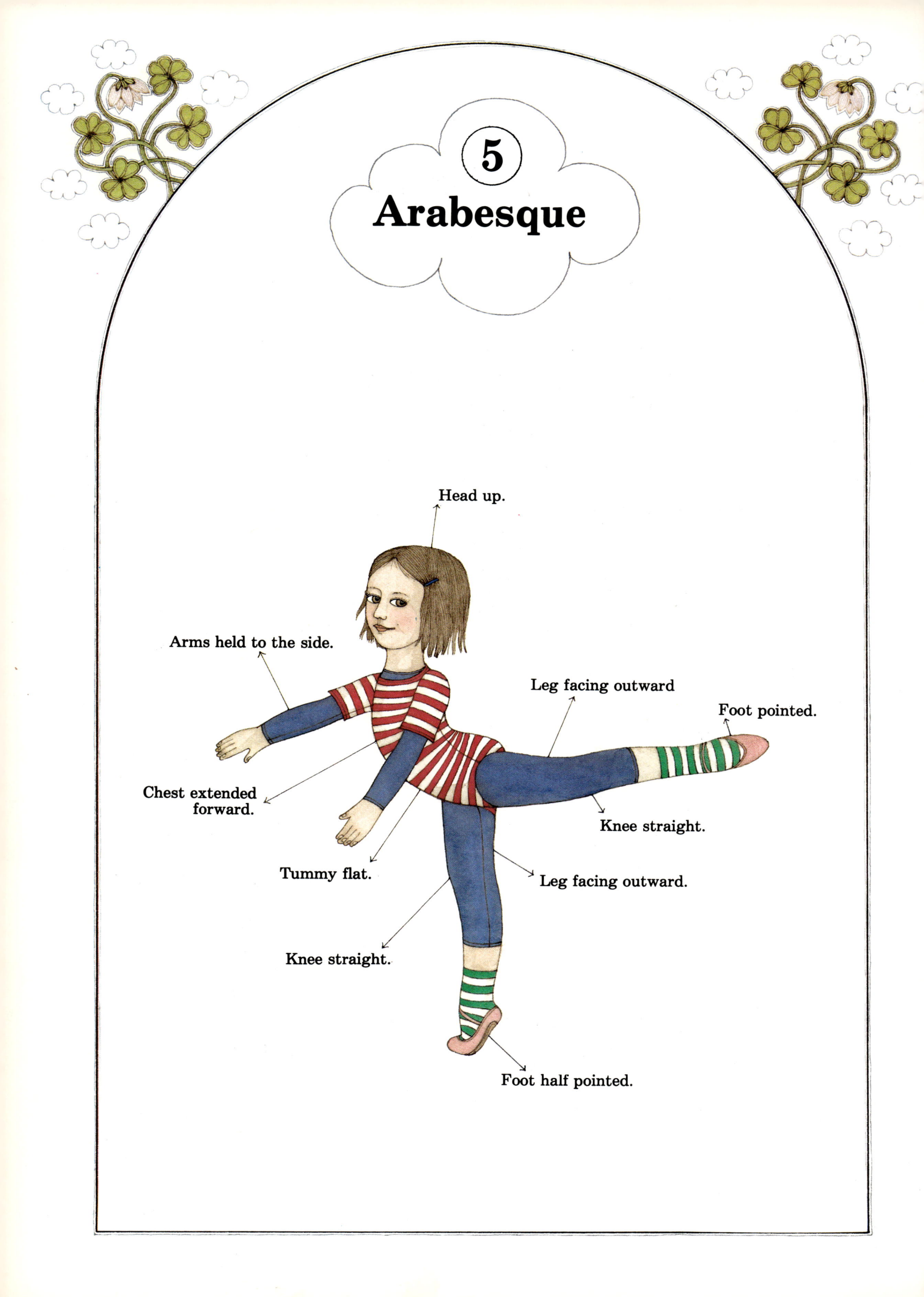

Head up.

Arms held to the side.

Leg facing outward

Foot pointed.

Chest extended forward.

Knee straight.

Tummy flat.

Leg facing outward.

Knee straight.

Foot half pointed.

6
Little Jumps

Important!
Start every jump in a demi-plié.
Land after every jump in a demi-plié.
Always!

Or else from 2nd position.

From 1st position go into
a demi-plié and jump on the spot high
in the air. Straighten legs and point feet.
Land in a demi-plié lowering feet gently.
Press heels firmly to the ground.
Land as quietly as possible.

Knees straight.

Toes pointed.

Demi-plié.

1st position.

7
Changement

From 3rd position, right foot in front, demi-plié, jump high on the spot. Change feet in mid-air and with the left foot in front, gently land in 3rd position

8
Echappé

A little jump on the spot from 3rd position, right foot in front, demi-plié, into 2nd position, demi-plié, and back into 3rd position, left foot in front, demi-plié. Heels firmly on the ground. Keep upper body and arms very still.

9
Assemblé

A little jump from one leg on to two legs. 3rd position, left foot in front, demi-plié, slide right leg out to the side, jump high, and gently land in a demi-plié with both legs in 3rd position, right foot in front.

10
Grand jeté

Run 2 steps — right-left — slide right leg through 1st position forward and extend upwards. Jump high and wide as if you were jumping over a large puddle. Land on the right leg in a demi-plié, body facing forward, left leg still extended to the back.

Draw the left leg up through 1st position, make 2 steps — left-right — draw the left leg through jump and land on the left leg.

Head up.

Ballet is fun!

2nd position.

Tummy pulled in.

Leg straight.

Toes pointed.

Toes pointed.

Leg straight.

Phew!

11
The Splits

When all your muscles are fully trained and well warmed up, you can practise the splits. 3rd position, left foot in front, demi-plié, slide right leg out to the back, place hands on the floor. Stretch left leg out in front, bounce, and if possible do the splits and put arms in the 2nd position. To stand up, draw in the left leg, bring the right leg to the front, place right foot over the knee and stand up. The left leg closes in the back in 3rd position. Then practise the same on the other side.

By the way . . .

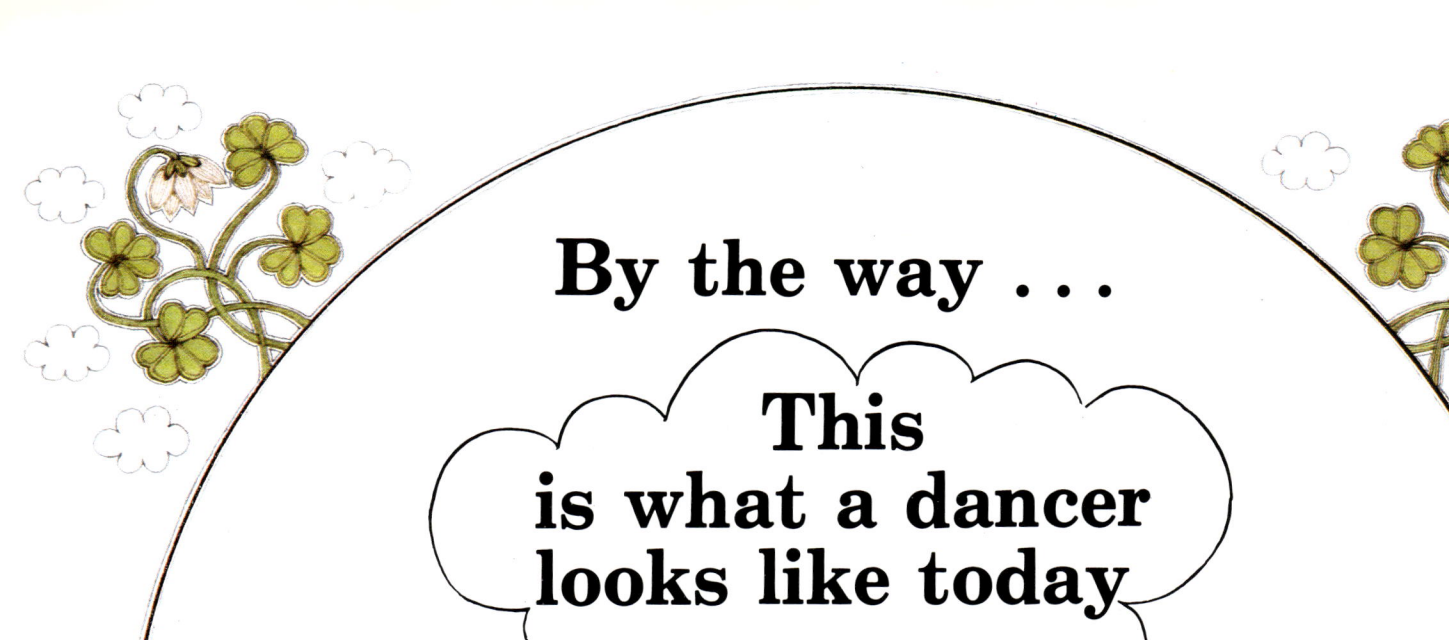

This is what a dancer looks like today

Here you can stick
a ballet photo
of yourself.

Little Ballet Dictionary
French-English

à coté ...... a koteh ...... sideways
adage ...... adarge ...... slowly
allegro ...... allehgro ...... fast
arabesque ...... arabesk ...... arabesque, ornament
assemblé ...... assamblay ...... join together
attitude ...... attitood ...... a standing position
balancé ...... balănssay ...... balanced
battement ...... batmăn ...... a beating movement
bras ...... bra ...... arm
chainés ...... shenay ...... series of small turning steps
changement ...... shanshmăn ...... change
cou-de-pied ...... koo deh peeay ...... ankle joint
coupé ...... kupeh ...... cut
croisé ...... krwahsay ...... crossed over
degagé ...... daygazhay ...... free or unconstrained
demi ...... demee ...... half
derrière ...... dehreeair ...... behind
dessous ...... dessoo ...... under
dessus ...... dessu ...... over
devant ...... dehvăn ...... in front
developpé ...... devellopay ...... an unfolding of the leg
échappé ...... ey-shah-pay ...... escape, break away
effacé ...... ehfahsay ...... turned to the side
en avant ...... ăn ăvan ...... forward
en dedans ...... ăn dehdăn ...... to the inside
en dehors ...... ăn deh-or ...... to the outside
en face ...... ăn fahss ...... facing
en suite ...... ăn sweet ...... in sequence
exercice ...... aychs-air-sees ...... exercise
fermer ...... fair-may ...... close
frappé ...... frah-pay ...... struck
glissade ...... glee-sahd ...... a slow, gliding step.
grand ...... grăn ...... large
grand jeté ...... grăn zhetay ...... large jump

For the pronunciation:
s ... pretty hard
zh, sh very soft
ss ... very hard
ăn ... spoken through the nose.

jambe	zhahmb	leg
jeté	zhetay	thrown, flung
ouvert	ouvehr	open
pas de basque	pa de bahsk	Basque step
pas de bourrée	pa de booray	Bourrée step
pas de chat	pa de sha	cat like step
passé	passay	pulled up
petit	peh-tee	little
pied	pee-ay	foot
pirouette	peer-oo-eht	a turn on the toe
plié	plee-ay	bent
pointe	pwãnt	point
port de bras	por dehbra	carriage of the arms
position	po-see-syon	position
preparation	pray-par-ahsyon	preparation
relever	reh-leh-vay	to rise up on the toes
révérence	ray-vair-ãns	bow
rond	rõn	round, circle
rond de jambe	rõn deh zhamb	circling the leg
simple	sahmpl	simple
sissonne	see-sonn	a jump from both legs on to one leg.
tendu	tawndu	taut, stretched
tête	teht	head
tomber	tombay	fall
tour	toor	turn
à la barre	ah la bar	at the barre
au milieu	oh meel-yuh	in the centre of the room

1	un	õn	one
2	deux	duh	two
3	trois	twa	three
4	quatre	kahtr	four
5	cinq	sank	five
6	six	seess	six
7	sept	set	seven
8	huit	weet	eight
9	neuf	nerf	nine
10	dix	deess	ten

> By the way . . .
> In French a pig
> is called cochon . . . koshõn.
> A cochonet . . . koshõnay . . .
> is a piglet.

About Us

Heidi Sievert chose the exercises for this book. Her father was a famous dancer. Her mother, Ossy Helken, has a ballet school in Frankfurt, West Germany. Heidi has danced ever since she could walk; by the time she was sixteen years old she was already in the Royal Ballet School in London. At nineteen she was the youngest prima ballerina in Germany and today she has a ballet school in Münster, West Germany.

Antje Vogel has painted since she's been able to think. This is her fourth book, others include *The Big Book for Growing Gardeners* and *There was once a Penguin*. She also danced at one time — for about ten years! Today she only dances from her desk to the stove, from the stove to her son and from her son back to her desk and, for her, that's a lot of fun!

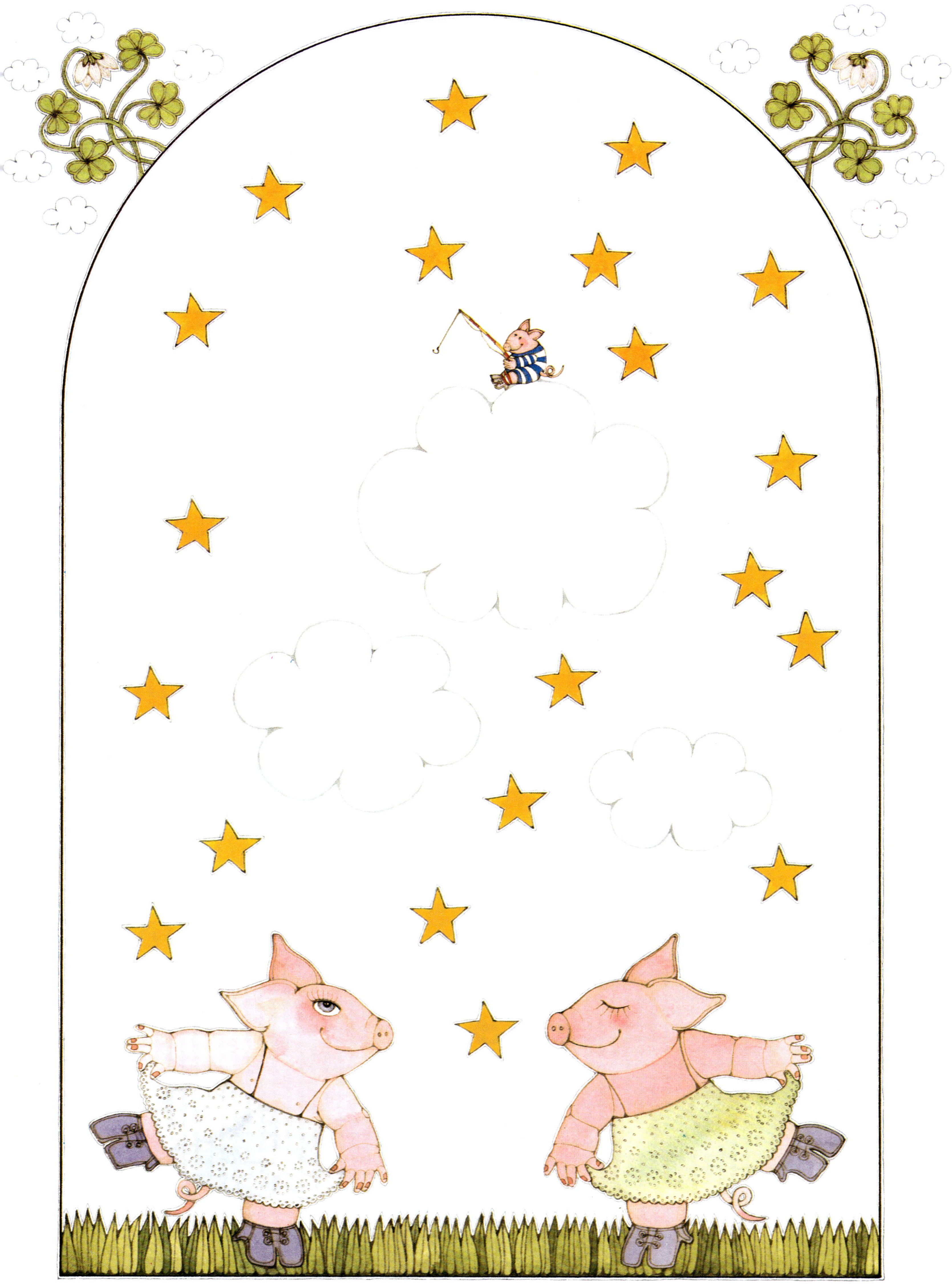

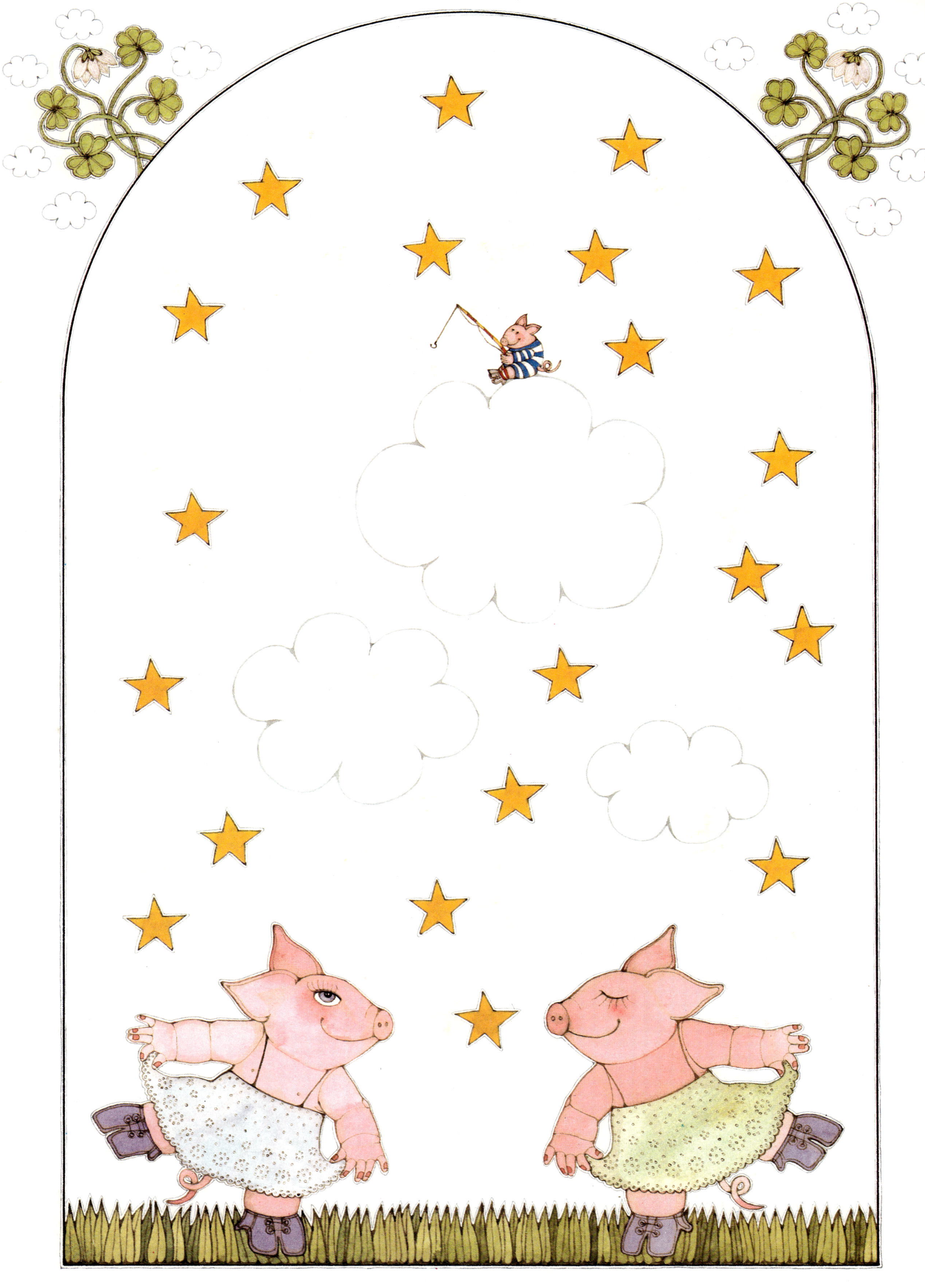